Examining the Claims of Jesus

Answers to Your Questions About Christ

DEE BRESTIN

SHAW BOOKS
an imprint of WATERBROOK PRESS

Examining the Claims of Jesus

A SHAW BOOK

PUBLISHED BY WATERBROOK PRESS

12265 Oracle Boulevard, Suite 200

Colorado Springs, Colorado 80921

A division of Random House, Inc.

ISBN 0-87788-246-0

Printed in the United States of America

2005

10 9 8 7 6 5 4 3 2 11

Contents

How to Use This Studyguide

F isherman studyguides are based on the inductive approach to Bible study. Inductive study is discovery study; we discover what the Bible says as we ask questions about its content and search for answers. This is quite different from the process in which a teacher *tells* a group *about* the Bible—what it means and what to do about it. In inductive study, God speaks directly to each of us through his Word.

A group functions best when a leader keeps the discussion on target, but the leader is neither the teacher nor the "answer person." A leader's responsibility is to *ask*—not *tell.* The answers come from the text itself as group members examine, discuss, and think together about the passage.

There are four kinds of questions in each study. The first is an *approach question.* Asked and answered before the Bible passage is read, this question breaks the ice and helps you start thinking about the topic of the Bible study. It begins to reveal where thoughts and feelings need to be transformed by Scripture.

Some of the earlier questions in each study are *observation questions*—who, what, where, when, and how—designed to help you learn some basic facts about the passage of Scripture.

Once you know what the Bible says, you need to ask, *What does it mean?* These *interpretation questions* help you discover the writer's basic message.

Next come *application questions,* which ask, *What does it mean to me?* They challenge you to live out the Scripture's life-transforming message.

Fisherman studyguides provide spaces between questions for jotting down responses as well as any related questions you would like to raise in the group. Each group member should have a copy of the studyguide and may take a turn in leading the group.

A group should use any accurate, modern translation of the Bible such as the *New International Version,* the *New American Standard Bible,* the *New Living Translation,* the *New Revised Standard Version,* the *New Jerusalem Bible,* or the *Good News Bible.* (Other translations or paraphrases of the Bible may be referred to when additional help is needed.) Bible commentaries should not be brought to a Bible study because they tend to dampen discussion and keep people from thinking for themselves.

Suggestions for Group Leaders

1. Thoroughly read and study the Bible passage before the meeting. Get a firm grasp on its themes and begin applying its teachings for yourself. Pray that the Holy Spirit will "guide you into all truth" (John 16:13) so that your leadership will guide others.

2. If any of the studyguide's questions seem ambiguous or unnatural to you, rephrase them, feeling free to add others that seem necessary to bring out the meaning of a verse.

3. Begin (and end) the study promptly. Start by asking someone to pray that every participant will both understand the passage and be open to its transforming power. Remember, the Holy Spirit is the teacher, not you!

4. Ask for volunteers to read the passages aloud.

5. As you ask the studyguide's questions in sequence, encourage everyone to participate in the discussion. If some are silent, try gently suggesting, "Let's have an answer from someone who hasn't spoken up yet."

6. If a question comes up that you can't answer, don't be afraid to admit that you're baffled. Assign the topic as a research project for someone to report on next week, or say, "I'll do some studying and let you know what I find out."

7. Keep the discussion moving, but be sure it stays focused. Though a certain number of tangents are inevitable, you'll want to quickly bring the discussion back to the topic at hand. Also, learn to pace the discussion so that you finish the lesson in the time allotted.

8. Don't be afraid of silences; some questions take time to answer, and some people need time to gather courage to speak. If silence persists, rephrase your question, but resist the temptation to answer it yourself.

9. If someone comes up with an answer that is clearly illogical or unbiblical, ask for further clarification: "What verse suggests that to you?"

10. Discourage overuse of cross references. Learn all you can from the passage at hand, while selectively incorporating a few important references suggested in the studyguide.

11. Some questions are marked with a ✎. This indicates that further information is available in the Leader's Notes at the back of the guide.

12. For more information on getting a new Bible study group started and keeping it functioning effectively, read *You Can Start a Bible Study Group* by Gladys M. Hunt and *Pilgrims in Progress: Growing Through Groups* by Jim and Carol Plueddemann. (Both books are available from Shaw Books.)

Suggestions for Group Members

1. Learn and apply the following ground rules for effective Bible study. (If new members join the group later, review these guidelines with the whole group.)

2. Remember that your goal is to learn all you can *from the Bible passage being studied.* Let it speak for itself without using Bible commentaries or other Bible passages. There is more than enough in each assigned passage to keep your group productively occupied for one session. Sticking to the passage saves the group from insecurity ("I don't have the right reference books—or the time to read anything else.") and confusion ("Where did *that* come from? I thought we were studying _____.").

3. Avoid the temptation to bring up those fascinating tangents that don't really grow out of the passage you are discussing. If the topic is of common interest, you can bring it up later in informal conversation after the study. Meanwhile, help one another stick to the subject.

4. Encourage one another to participate. People remember best what they discover and verbalize for

themselves. Some people are naturally shy, while others may be afraid of making a mistake. If your discussion is free and friendly and you show real interest in what other group members think and feel, the quieter ones will be more likely to speak up. Remember, the more people involved in a discussion, the richer it will be.

5. Guard yourself from answering too many questions or talking too much. Give others a chance to share their ideas. If you are one who participates easily, discipline yourself by counting to ten before you open your mouth.

6. Make personal, honest applications and commit yourself to letting God's Word change you.

Introduction

A short beginner's studyguide based on the first five chapters of John? With the Scripture text included? It's about time!

This studyguide explores John because it was written with a specific purpose: "that you may believe that Jesus is the Christ, the Son of God, and that by believing you may have life in his name" (John 20:31).

Why is it so important to take a careful look at Jesus's life? Because Jesus made some extraordinary claims. He claimed to be far more than a religious teacher or a revolutionary. He claimed that lives would be changed when people received him for who he was. Only as we examine his claims and study his life can we come to know his *person* and what his life means to us now.

This studyguide includes a study from the book of Romans that clarifies the basics of the Christian faith. Another study, from First Peter, offers instruction in the life of faith—the Christian's identity and purpose. These are optional studies, designed to continue the theme of the John studies as well as to allow time to order more studyguides for those who wish to continue. (We recommend *1, 2, 3 John: How Should a Christian Live?* or *Mark: God in Action*.)

Scripture text is included in the pages of this studyguide. Those people who are new at Bible study may not have Bibles readily available. Also, with everyone using the same translation, confusion will be minimized. And everyone will have the advantage of using the *New International Version* and *The Living Bible* (in different studies), chosen for their elements of accuracy, clarity, and contemporary language.

May God be with you as you begin the adventure of discovering who Jesus is.

Who Is Jesus?

JOHN 1

A t Christmas, carolers sing, "Word of the Father, now in flesh appearing." "The Word" is just one of many names that are given to Jesus in the Bible to describe his various characteristics and the purposes of his life and ministry. "The Word" is how John referred to Jesus in this passage.

Why would Jesus be called the Word? One reason is that God has chosen to *communicate* through him. God became flesh—he became a man—so that he could tell us about himself and instruct us about our lives. Words are also a way of *connecting* with another person; Jesus bridged the gap between God the Father and us. Another awe-inspiring reason Jesus is called the Word is because he, with God and the Holy Spirit, created the world by *speaking* it into existence.

1. List some of the reasons you have used words in the past twenty-four hours.

What insight does this give you into Jesus being
called "the Word"?

Read Aloud John 1:1-3.

[1]In the beginning was the Word, and the Word was with
God, and the Word was God. [2]He was with God in the
beginning.
[3]Through him all things were made; without him
nothing was made that has been made.

2. List the facts about Jesus *(the Word)* that John listed
    in these verses.

3. According to John, how long has Jesus existed?
    What was Jesus doing in the beginning?

4. Was it clear to you before now that God the *Son* as
    well as God the Father created the world? What
    effect, if any, does this have on your view of Jesus?

READ JOHN 1:4-8.

⁴In him was life, and that life was the light of men.
⁵The light shines in the darkness, but the darkness has
not understood it.
    ⁶There came a man who was sent from God; his
name was John. ⁷He came as a witness to testify concerning that light, so that through him all men might believe.
⁸He himself was not the light; he came only as a witness
to the light.

5. What do you learn about Jesus as the light?

    Give an example of how the world in its darkness
    has failed to understand or overcome the light of
    Jesus.

6. What are some functions and characteristics of
    light? How can these be seen in Jesus?

⌒ 7. Why might coming to the light of Jesus be painful?
In what areas of life do people avoid "light"?

READ JOHN 1:9-13.

⁹The true light that gives light to every man was coming
into the world.

¹⁰He was in the world, and though the world was
made through him, the world did not recognize him.
¹¹He came to that which was his own, but his own did not
receive him. ¹²Yet to all who received him, to those who
believed in his name, he gave the right to become children
of God—¹³children born not of natural descent, nor of
human decision or a husband's will, but born of God.

8. What is the irony in verse 10? What evidence do
you see that the world still doesn't recognize Jesus?

✎ 9. How does verse 12 contrast with verse 11? As you consider verses 12 and 13, what do you think it means to become a child of God?

READ JOHN 1:14-18.

[14]The Word became flesh and made his dwelling among us. We have seen his glory, the glory of the One and Only, who came from the Father, full of grace and truth.

[15]John testifies concerning him. He cries out, saying, "This was he of whom I said, 'He who comes after me has surpassed me because he was before me.'" [16]From the fullness of his grace we have all received one blessing after another. [17]For the law was given through Moses; grace and truth came through Jesus Christ. [18]No one has ever seen God, but God the One and Only, who is at the Father's side, has made him known.

10. Verse 16 says that grace (undeserved favor) is the basis of blessings in our lives. Give an example of this from your experience.

What purpose of Jesus's life is revealed in verse 18?

READ JOHN 1:19-34.

[19]Now this was John's testimony when the Jews of Jerusalem sent priests and Levities to ask him who he was. [20]He did not fail to confess, but confessed freely, "I am not the Christ."

[21]They asked him, "Then who are you? Are you Elijah?"

He said, "I am not."

"Are you the Prophet?"

He answered, "No."

[22]Finally they said, "Who are you? Give us an answer to take back to those who sent us. What do you say about yourself?"

[23]John replied in the words of Isaiah the prophet, "I am the voice of one calling in the desert, 'Make straight the way for the Lord.'"

[24]Now some Pharisees who had been sent [25]questioned him, "Why then do you baptize if you are not the Christ, nor Elijah, nor the Prophet?"

[26]"I baptize with water," John replied, "but among you stands one you do not know. [27]He is the one who comes after me, the thongs of whose sandals I am not worthy to untie."

[28]This all happened at Bethany on the other side of the Jordan, where John was baptizing.

[29]The next day John saw Jesus coming toward him and said, "Look, the Lamb of God, who takes away the sin of the world! [30]This is the one I meant when I said, 'A man who comes after me has surpassed me because he was before me.' [31]I myself did not know him, but the reason I came baptizing with water was that he might be revealed to Israel."

[32]Then John gave this testimony: "I saw the Spirit come down from heaven as a dove and remain on him. [33]I would not have known him, except that the one who sent me to baptize with water told me, 'The man on whom you see the Spirit come down and remain is he who will baptize with the Holy Spirit.' [34]I have seen and I testify that this is the Son of God."

11. What did John the Baptist recognize about Jesus? about himself?

According to John the Baptist, what was Jesus's purpose (verse 29)?

12. How did John know who Jesus was (verses 32-33)?

READ JOHN 1:35-51.

[35]The next day John was there again with two of his disciples. [36]When he saw Jesus passing by, he said, "Look, the Lamb of God!"

[37]When the two disciples heard him say this, they followed Jesus. [38]Turning around, Jesus saw them following and asked, "What do you want?"

They said, "Rabbi" (which means Teacher), "where are you staying?"

[39]"Come," he replied, "and you will see."

So they went and saw where he was staying, and spent that day with him. It was about the tenth hour.

[40]Andrew, Simon Peter's brother, was one of the two who heard what John had said and who had followed Jesus. [41]The first thing Andrew did was to find his brother Simon and tell him, "We have found the Messiah" (that is, the Christ). [42]And he brought him to Jesus.

Jesus looked at him and said, "You are Simon son of John. You will be called Cephas" (which, when translated, is Peter).

[43]The next day Jesus decided to leave for Galilee. Finding Philip, he said to him, "Follow me."

[44]Philip, like Andrew and Peter, was from the town of Bethsaida. [45]Philip found Nathanael and told him, "We have found the one Moses wrote about in the Law, and about whom the prophets also wrote—Jesus of Nazareth, the son of Joseph."

[46]"Nazareth! Can anything good come from there?" Nathanael asked.

"Come and see," said Philip.

⁴⁷When Jesus saw Nathanael approaching, he said of him, "Here is a true Israelite, in whom there is nothing false."

⁴⁸"How do you know me?" Nathanael asked.

Jesus answered, "I saw you while you were still under the fig tree before Philip called you."

⁴⁹Then Nathanael declared, "Rabbi, you are the Son of God; you are the King of Israel."

⁵⁰Jesus said, "You believe because I told you I saw you under the fig tree. You shall see greater things than that."

⁵¹He then added, "I tell you the truth, you shall see heaven open, and the angels of God ascending and descending on the Son of Man."

13. Describe what each of the following men knew about Jesus:

Andrew (verses 40-41)

Philip (verse 45)

Nathanael (verses 46-51)

14. What have you learned about Jesus from this study that you didn't know before?

In what ways, if any, does this new information change or enhance your views of Jesus?

STUDY 2

More About Jesus

JOHN 2

G od has communicated with us throughout history, giving instructions for good living and warnings against
patterns that will harm us. But what is God like? After centuries
of giving information about himself through the prophets, God
decided to *show* us himself in human form. Thus, Jesus came
to earth as a person. Colossians 2:9 says that "in Christ all the
fullness of the Deity lives in bodily form." In the second chapter of John, we see two sides of Jesus: his concern and compassion for individuals, and his holy anger, both of which
reflect God's character.

1. Think of someone you know well. What kinds of
   situations have revealed to you the character of that
   person?

READ JOHN 2:1-11.

¹On the third day a wedding took place at Cana in Galilee. Jesus' mother was there, ²and Jesus and his disciples had also been invited to the wedding. ³When the wine was gone, Jesus' mother said to him, "They have no more wine."

⁴"Dear woman, why do you involve me?" Jesus replied. "My time has not yet come."

⁵His mother said to the servants, "Do whatever he tells you."

⁶Nearby stood six stone water jars, the kind used by the Jews for ceremonial washing, each holding from twenty to thirty gallons.

⁷Jesus said to the servants, "Fill the jars with water"; so they filled them to the brim.

⁸Then he told them, "Now draw some out and take it to the master of the banquet."

They did so, ⁹and the master of the banquet tasted the water that had been turned into wine. He did not realize where it had come from, though the servants who had drawn the water knew. Then he called the bridegroom aside ¹⁰and said, "Everyone brings out the choice wine first and then the cheaper wine after the guests have had too much to drink; but you have saved the best till now."

¹¹This, the first of his miraculous signs, Jesus performed at Cana in Galilee. He thus revealed his glory, and his disciples put their faith in him.

2. Jesus's mother saw a problem. What was it, and why did she come to Jesus?

   What can we learn from Mary's response to Jesus (verse 5)?

3. How would you have felt if you had been the host at the wedding reception?

4. Describe what Jesus did, how the servants responded to him, and the quality of the wine.

5. What do you learn from this incident about Jesus's personal concern for people?

6. Share with the group a time when God's provision was particularly clear and personal to you (such as an answer to prayer, God's protection in a time of danger, or another example).

✐ READ JOHN 2:12-17.

[12]After this he went down to Capernaum with his mother and brothers and his disciples. There they stayed for a few days.

[13]When it was almost time for the Jewish Passover, Jesus went up to Jerusalem. [14]In the temple courts he found men selling cattle, sheep and doves, and others sitting at tables exchanging money. [15]So he made a whip out of cords, and drove all from the temple area, both sheep and cattle; he scattered the coins of the money changers and overturned their tables. [16]To those who sold doves he said, "Get these out of here! How dare you turn my Father's house into a market!"

[17]His disciples remembered that it is written: "Zeal for your house will consume me."

7. How had the temple worship become corrupted? What was Jesus's reaction to this?

8. What significance do you see in the fact that Jesus made a whip instead of simply grabbing one?

What did he say to the "religious" men?

9. Why was Jesus so angry? What about our worship services today might also make him angry?

10. Why doesn't God overlook sin? Explain how it is possible for God to be both loving and angry.

READ JOHN 2:18-25.

[18]Then the Jews demanded of him, "What miraculous sign can you show us to prove your authority to do all this?"

[19]Jesus answered them, "Destroy this temple, and I will raise it again in three days."

[20]The Jews replied, "It has taken forty-six years to build this temple, and you are going to raise it in three days?" [21]But the temple he had spoken of was his body. [22]After he was raised from the dead, his disciples recalled what he had said. Then they believed the Scripture and the words that Jesus had spoken.

[23]Now while he was in Jerusalem at the Passover Feast, many people saw the miraculous signs he was doing and believed in his name. [24]But Jesus would not entrust himself to them, for he knew all men. [25]He did not need man's testimony about man, for he knew what was in a man.

11. How did the Jews react to Jesus's anger? What riddle did Jesus give them? What did the Jews think he meant?

12. What did Jesus really mean? This prediction was later fulfilled in Jesus's death and resurrection. What did Jesus's knowledge of future events indicate about him?

13. What aspects of your life do you think Jesus views with compassion? with holy anger?

Jesus Gives Eternal Life

JOHN 3

T he terms saved and *born again* are often used flippantly to describe everything from retreaded tires to religious fanatics. Actually, they represent important scriptural concepts. Perhaps the resistance to these terms is more a reaction to the way they have been presented (and sometimes abused) than to what they actually mean. Before Jesus was born, the angel told Joseph to name Mary's baby Jesus because "he will save his people from their sins" (Matthew 1:21). In this passage, we learn the origin of the term *born again.*

It is sometimes possible to exist in a church atmosphere without understanding the central beliefs of Christianity. Throughout history, many religious systems have been unable to help individuals prepare for death and eternity. Such was the situation of Nicodemus. Though a religious leader, he did not comprehend how to receive eternal life. But one night Nicodemus came to Jesus with a heart that desired to understand.

1. Imagine that you have just been born. What are the positive elements of being a brand-new human being? What are some of the challenges?

READ JOHN 3:1-3.

[1]Now there was a man of the Pharisees named Nicodemus, a member of the Jewish ruling council. [2]He came to Jesus at night and said, "Rabbi, we know you are a teacher who has come from God. For no one could perform the miraculous signs you are doing if God were not with him."

[3]In reply Jesus declared, "I tell you the truth, no one can see the kingdom of God unless he is born again."

2. What set Jesus apart from ordinary religious teachers?

Why do you think Nicodemus came to Jesus at night?

3. Look at Jesus's reply. What unspoken question in Nicodemus's heart do you think he was answering? What did he mean by *seeing the kingdom of God?*

READ JOHN 3:4-8.

[4]"How can a man be born when he is old?" Nicodemus asked. "Surely he cannot enter a second time into his mother's womb to be born!"

[5]Jesus answered, "I tell you the truth, no one can enter the kingdom of God unless he is born of water and the Spirit. [6]Flesh gives birth to flesh, but the Spirit gives birth to spirit. [7]You should not be surprised at my saying 'You must be born again.' [8]The wind blows wherever it pleases. You hear its sound, but you cannot tell where it comes from or where it is going. So it is with everyone born of the Spirit."

4. How was Nicodemus's attitude different from that of the "religious" people in John 2? In what way did this benefit him?

5. What did Nicodemus think Jesus meant by the words "born again"? How did Jesus explain the difference between physical and spiritual birth?

✐ 6. Often people debate whether spiritual birth is an event or a process. (In other words, is it something that happens suddenly or are there a series of steps?) Insight can be gained by comparing it to pregnancy, birth, and maturation. What similarities do you see?

What other similarities do you see between physical and spiritual birth?

Read John 3:9-15 and Numbers 21:5-9.

(*Note:* The passage in Numbers contains the incident Jesus referred to in John 3:14.)

9"How can this be?" Nicodemus asked.

10"You are Israel's teacher," said Jesus, "and do you not understand these things? 11I tell you the truth, we speak of what we know, and we testify to what we have seen, but still you people do not accept our testimony. 12I have spoken to you of earthly things and you do not believe; how then will you believe if I speak of heavenly things? [13]No one has ever gone into heaven except the one who came from heaven—the Son of Man. [14]Just as Moses lifted up the snake in the desert, so the Son of Man must be lifted up, [15]that everyone who believes in him may have eternal life." (John 3:9-15)

[5][The people] spoke against God… "Why have you brought us up out of Egypt to die in the desert? There is no bread! There is no water! And we detest this miserable food!"

[6]Then the LORD sent venomous snakes among them; they bit the people and many Israelites died. [7]The people came to Moses and said, "We sinned when we spoke against the LORD and against you. Pray that the LORD will take the snakes away from us." So Moses prayed for the people.

[8]The LORD said to Moses, "Make a snake and put it up on a pole; anyone who is bitten can look at it and live." [9]So Moses made a bronze snake and put it up on a pole. Then when anyone was bitten by a snake and looked at the bronze snake, he lived. (Numbers 21:5-9)

7. What do you think happened to the Israelites who refused to look at the bronze snake? What do you think happened to those who admitted their sin and looked at it?

How was faith in God at work here? What was the result of this faith?

8. Summarize in your own words what Jesus said in John 3:14-15: "Just as Moses lifted up the snake in the desert, so the Son of Man must be lifted up, that everyone who believes in him may have eternal life."

How was Jesus *lifted up?*

What promise did he give to those who place their faith in him and his death on the cross (John 3:15)?

9. Some say it is simplistic to think that we can receive new life (eternal life) simply by placing our trust in Jesus and his sacrifice on the cross. Instead of trusting Jesus, they try to "earn" their way to heaven. Based on Jesus's illustration of the serpent, what would you tell them?

Read John 3:16-21.

¹⁶For God so loved the world that he gave his one and only Son, that whoever believes in him shall not perish but have eternal life. ¹⁷For God did not send his Son into the world to condemn the world, but to save the world through him. ¹⁸Whoever believes in him is not condemned, but whoever does not believe stands condemned already because he has not believed in the name of God's one and only Son. ¹⁹This is the verdict: Light has come into the world, but men loved darkness instead of light because their deeds were evil. ²⁰Everyone who does evil hates the light, and will not come into the light for fear that his deeds will be exposed. ²¹But whoever lives by the truth comes into the light, so that it may be seen plainly that what he has done has been done through God.

10. John 3:16 has been called the most important verse in the Bible because it is the heart of God's message to humanity. What do you learn in this verse about God? about Jesus? about *whomever?*

11. Why do some refuse to come to Jesus (verses 19-21)? What changes might you expect to see in the

life of someone who has repented and believed in Jesus?

Read John 3:22-36.

22After this, Jesus and his disciples went out into the Judean countryside, where he spent some time with them, and baptized. 23Now John also was baptizing at Aenon near Salim, because there was plenty of water, and people were constantly coming to be baptized. 24(This was before John was put in prison.) 25An argument developed between some of John's disciples and a certain Jew over the matter of ceremonial washing. 26They came to John and said to him, "Rabbi, that man who was with you on the other side of the Jordan—the one you testified about—well, he is baptizing, and everyone is going to him."

27To this John replied, "A man can receive only what is given him from heaven. 28You yourselves can testify that I said, 'I am not the Christ but am sent ahead of him.' 29The bride belongs to the bridegroom. The friend who attends the bridegroom waits and listens for him, and is full of joy when he hears the bridegroom's voice. That joy is mine, and it is now complete. 30He must become greater; I must become less.

31"The one who comes from above is above all; the one who is from the earth belongs to the earth, and speaks as one from the earth. The one who comes from heaven is above all. [32]He testifies to what he has seen and heard, but no one accepts his testimony. [33]The man who has accepted it has certified that God is truthful. [34]For the one whom God has sent speaks the words of God, for God gives the Spirit without limit. [35]The Father loves the Son and has placed everything in his hands. [36]Whoever believes in the Son has eternal life, but whoever rejects the Son will not see life, for God's wrath remains on him."

12.   Describe the shift in John's relationship with Jesus. Which verse sums up John's position?

13.   What are the two alternatives given in verse 36?

How is God's anger one aspect of his love toward us?

14.   If you have received new spiritual life, what have been some of the positive elements of that change?

Jesus Satisfies Our Longings

JOHN 4

S aint Augustine said, "You made us for yourself, O God, and our hearts are restless until they find their rest in you." Every person has spiritual longings. Many try to satisfy this heart need with material possessions, alcohol, professional success, or even occult practices, such as witchcraft and astrology. Sometimes we aren't sure, ourselves, just what we turn to for fulfillment, until someone helps us see ourselves. Jesus had a way of opening the eyes of people—and guiding them to what really satisfies.

1. List some of the ways people try to satisfy their longings, only to find their efforts backfiring. Why do you think so many people are still searching well into their adult years?

Read John 4:1-15.

[1]The Pharisees heard that Jesus was gaining and baptizing more disciples than John, [2]although in fact it was not Jesus who baptized, but his disciples. [3]When the Lord learned of this, he left Judea and went back once more to Galilee.

[4]Now he had to go through Samaria. [5]So he came to a town in Samaria called Sychar, near the plot of ground Jacob had given to his son Joseph. [6]Jacob's well was there, and Jesus, tired as he was from the journey, sat down by the well. It was about the sixth hour.

[7]When a Samaritan woman came to draw water, Jesus said to her, "Will you give me a drink?" [8](His disciples had gone into the town to buy food.)

[9]The Samaritan woman said to him, "You are a Jew and I am a Samaritan woman. How can you ask me for a drink?" (For Jews do not associate with Samaritans.)

[10]Jesus answered her, "If you knew the gift of God and who it is that asks you for a drink, you would have asked him and he would have given you living water."

[11]"Sir," the woman said, "you have nothing to draw with and the well is deep. Where can you get this living water? [12]Are you greater than our father Jacob, who gave us the well and drank from it himself, as did also his sons and his flocks and herds?"

[13]Jesus answered, "Everyone who drinks this water will be thirsty again, [14]but whoever drinks the water I give him will never thirst. Indeed, the water I give him will become in him a spring of water welling up to eternal life."

¹⁵The woman said to him, "Sir, give me this water so that I won't get thirsty and have to keep coming here to draw water."

✎ 2. Why was the woman surprised that Jesus spoke to her?

✎ 3. What two kinds of water did Jesus talk about? How were they similar? How were they different?

4. Except for Christianity, all major religions teach that we must work our way to heaven. How is what Jesus taught here different?

5. How do you know whether the woman recognized Jesus as God? How well did she grasp what he meant by "living water"?

READ JOHN 4:16-26.

¹⁶He told her, "Go, call your husband and come back."

¹⁷"I have no husband," she replied.

Jesus said to her, "You are right when you say you

have no husband. [18]The fact is, you have had five husbands, and the man you now have is not your husband. What you have just said is quite true."

[19]"Sir," the woman said, "I can see that you are a prophet. [20]Our fathers worshiped on this mountain, but you Jews claim that the place where we must worship is in Jerusalem."

[21]Jesus declared, "Believe me, woman, a time is coming when you will worship the Father neither on this mountain nor in Jerusalem. [22]You Samaritans worship what you do not know; we worship what we do know, for salvation is from the Jews. [23]Yet a time is coming and has now come when the true worshipers will worship the Father in spirit and truth, for they are the kind of worshipers the Father seeks. [24]God is spirit, and his worshipers must worship in spirit and in truth."

[25]The woman said, "I know that Messiah" (called Christ) "is coming. When he comes, he will explain everything to us."

[26]Then Jesus declared, "I who speak to you am he."

6. How did Jesus zero in on the woman's problem?

7. How much did Jesus know about her life? If Jesus were to sit down with you, what might he point out in your life as futile attempts to fulfill your longings?

8. How did the woman try to change the subject?
    Why might she have been nervous about letting
    Jesus get to the heart of the matter?

9. In verses 21-24 Jesus told the woman what is
    important to God about worship. How did Jesus
    show the woman that the location of worship is
    not what is important to God?

10. What does the Father want from us in worship?

    What would it mean for your worship of God to be
    based on truth?

11. Based on the woman's statement in verse 25, what
    question do you think was in her mind? How did
    Jesus clear away her confusion?

Read John 4:27-42.

27Just then his disciples returned and were surprised to find him talking with a woman. But no one asked, "What do you want?" or "Why are you talking with her?"

28Then, leaving her water jar, the woman went back to the town and said to the people, 29"Come, see a man who told me everything I ever did. Could this be the Christ?" 30They came out of the town and made their way toward him.

31Meanwhile his disciples urged him, "Rabbi, eat something."

32But he said to them, "I have food to eat that you know nothing about."

33Then his disciples said to each other, "Could someone have brought him food?"

34"My food," said Jesus, "is to do the will of him who sent me and to finish his work. 35Do you not say, 'Four months more and then the harvest'? I tell you, open your eyes and look at the fields! They are ripe for harvest. 36Even now the reaper draws his wages, even now he harvests the crop for eternal life, so that the sower and the reaper may be glad together. 37Thus the saying 'One sows and another reaps' is true. 38I sent you to reap what you have not worked for. Others have done the hard work, and you have reaped the benefits of their labor."

39Many of the Samaritans from that town believed in him because of the woman's testimony, "He told me everything I ever did." 40So when the Samaritans came to him, they urged him to stay with them, and he stayed two days. 41And because of his words many more became believers.

⁴²They said to the woman, "We no longer believe just because of what you said; now we have heard for ourselves, and we know that this man really is the Savior of the world."

12. How did the woman demonstrate her decreasing interest in physical water and her increasing interest in spiritual water?

13. Who did the Samaritans think Jesus was? Why?

Read John 4:43-54.

⁴³After the two days he left for Galilee. ⁴⁴(Now Jesus himself had pointed out that a prophet has no honor in his own country.) ⁴⁵When he arrived in Galilee, the Galileans welcomed him. They had seen all that he had done in Jerusalem at the Passover Feast, for they also had been there.

⁴⁶Once more he visited Cana in Galilee, where he had turned the water into wine. And there was a certain royal official whose son lay sick at Capernaum. ⁴⁷When this man heard that Jesus had arrived in Galilee from Judea, he went to him and begged him to come and heal his son, who was close to death.

[48]"Unless you people see miraculous signs and wonders," Jesus told him, "you will never believe."

[49]The royal official said, "Sir, come down before my child dies."

[50]Jesus replied, "You may go. Your son will live."

The man took Jesus at his word and departed. [51]While he was still on the way, his servants met him with the news that his boy was living. [52]When he inquired as to the time when his son got better, they said to him, "The fever left him yesterday at the seventh hour."

[53]Then the father realized that this was the exact time at which Jesus had said to him, "Your son will live." So he and all his household believed.

[54]This was the second miraculous sign that Jesus performed, having come from Judea to Galilee.

14. Faith and action form a circle. How is this demonstrated by this incident?

15. According to the faith you have at this time, what kind of action are you able to take?

Responding to Jesus

JOHN 5

ost of us have experienced those "Aha!" moments when we are suddenly illuminated to a reality we haven't known or understood before.

The real test of our character, however, is not in the discovery itself but in our response to it. How is my life different now that I have received new information?

1. Recall a discovery—big or small—that has had a lasting impact on your life.

READ JOHN 5:1-8.

¹Some time later, Jesus went up to Jerusalem for a feast of the Jews. ²Now there is in Jerusalem near the Sheep Gate a

pool, which in Aramaic is called Bethesda and which is
surrounded by five covered colonnades. [3]Here a great
number of disabled people used to lie—the blind, the
lame, the paralyzed—(and they waited for the moving of
the waters. [4]From time to time an angel of the Lord would
come down and stir up the waters. The first one into the
pool after each such disturbance would be cured of whatever disease he had.)* [5]One who was there had been an
invalid for thirty-eight years. [6]When Jesus saw him lying
there and learned that he had been in this condition for a
long time, he asked him, "Do you want to get well?"

[7]"Sir," the invalid replied, "I have no one to help me
into the pool when the water is stirred. While I am trying
to get in, someone else goes down ahead of me."

[8]Then Jesus said to him, "Get up! Pick up your mat
and walk."

✎ 2.   Describe the scene at the pool of Bethesda.

How long had the man been an invalid? Why
would Jesus ask the question he did?

---

* *Some less important manuscripts include the words in parentheses.*

3. If you were offered an instant cure after being
    bedridden for many years, what fears might you
    have about the changes it would bring to your life?

    Are there people who don't want to get well spiritu-
    ally? Give reasons for your answer.

4. What did Jesus ask the sick man to do? How did
    Jesus make it possible for him to obey?

READ JOHN 5:9-16.

⁹At once the man was cured; he picked up his mat and
walked.
    The day on which this took place was a Sabbath,
¹⁰and so the Jews said to the man who had been healed,
"It is the Sabbath; the law forbids you to carry your mat."

[11]But he replied, "The man who made me well said to me, 'Pick up your mat and walk.'"

[12]So they asked him, "Who is this fellow who told you to pick it up and walk?"

[13]The man who was healed had no idea who it was, for Jesus had slipped away into the crowd that was there.

[14]Later Jesus found him at the temple and said to him, "See, you are well again. Stop sinning or something worse may happen to you." [15]The man went away and told the Jews that it was Jesus who had made him well.

[16]So, because Jesus was doing these things on the Sabbath, the Jews persecuted him.

5. Describe the religious leaders' feelings about Jesus's act of compassion.

Contrast their attitude toward the healed man with Jesus's attitude. What motives did they have for wanting to know who had healed him?

6. What evidence do you find that the healed man lacked an interest in Jesus or gratitude (verses 13,15)? What warning did Jesus give him (verse 14)?

READ JOHN 5:17-30.

[17]Jesus said to them, "My Father is always at his work to this very day, and I, too, am working." [18]For this reason the Jews tried all the harder to kill him; not only was he breaking the Sabbath, but he was even calling God his own Father, making himself equal with God.

[19]Jesus gave them this answer: "I tell you the truth, the Son can do nothing by himself; he can do only what he sees his Father doing, because whatever the Father does the Son also does. [20]For the Father loves the Son and shows him all he does. Yes, to your amazement he will show him even greater things than these. [21]For just as the Father raises the dead and gives them life, even so the Son gives life to whom he is pleased to give it. [22]Moreover, the Father judges no one, but has entrusted all judgment to the Son, [23]that all may honor the Son just as they honor the Father. He who does not honor the Son does not honor the Father, who sent him.

[24]"I tell you the truth, whoever hears my word and believes him who sent me has eternal life and will not be condemned; he has crossed over from death to life. [25]I tell you the truth, a time is coming and has now come when the dead will hear the voice of the Son of God and those who hear will live. [26]For as the Father has life in himself, so he has granted the Son to have life in himself. [27]And he has given him authority to judge because he is the Son of Man.

[28]"Do not be amazed at this, for a time is coming when all who are in their graves will hear his voice [29]and come out—those who have done good will rise to live,

and those who have done evil will rise to be condemned.
³⁰By myself I can do nothing; I judge only as I hear, and
my judgment is just, for I seek not to please myself but
him who sent me."

7. In the first chapter of John, the gospel writer claims
that Jesus is God. Here Jesus himself made the same
claim. What do the following verses show about
Jesus's relationship with his Father?

verses 17-18

verse 19

verse 20

verse 21

verse 23

verse 30

✐ 8. Give the two reasons the Jews wanted to kill Jesus (verse 18).

✐ 9. How will our choices in this life affect our destiny after death (verses 28-29)? What part do faith and obedience play in "doing good"?

READ JOHN 5:31-47.

³¹"If I testify about myself, my testimony is not valid. ³²There is another who testifies in my favor, and I know that his testimony about me is valid.

³³"You have sent to John and he has testified to the truth. ³⁴Not that I accept human testimony; but I mention it that you may be saved. ³⁵John was a lamp that burned and gave light, and you chose for a time to enjoy his light.

³⁶"I have testimony weightier than that of John. For the very work that the Father has given me to finish, and which I am doing, testifies that the Father has sent me.

[37]And the Father who sent me has himself testified concerning me. You have never heard his voice nor seen his form, [38]nor does his word dwell in you, for you do not believe the one he sent. [39]You diligently study the Scriptures because you think that by them you possess eternal life. These are the Scriptures that testify about me, [40]yet you refuse to come to me to have life.

[41]"I do not accept praise from men, [42]but I know you. I know that you do not have the love of God in your hearts. [43]I have come in my Father's name, and you do not accept me; but if someone else comes in his own name, you will accept him. [44]How can you believe if you accept praise from one another, yet make no effort to obtain the praise that comes from the only God?

[45]"But do not think I will accuse you before the Father. Your accuser is Moses, on whom your hopes are set. [46]If you believed Moses, you would believe me, for he wrote about me. [47]But since you do not believe what he wrote, how are you going to believe what I say?"

10. The Jews were responding to Jesus with unbelief, despite many evidences that he was who he claimed to be. Examine each of the following statements of Jesus and list those who gave evidence that his claims were true:

verses 33-35 (this is John the Baptist, not John the gospel writer)

verse 36

verse 37

verse 39

verse 46

11. Obviously, the Jews' problem was not a lack of evidence. What was their root problem (verse 42)? What evidence of their hardheartedness have you seen in this chapter?

Contrast their attitude with inquirers such as Nicodemus and the woman at the well.

🖎 12. On the basis of these first five chapters in John's gospel, write down some of the evidence you have seen that supports Jesus's claim of being God.

13. What are your thoughts about Jesus at this point?

What are your questions?

The following is an explanation of the central message of the Bible. Read it carefully for understanding. Take fifteen or twenty minutes to think this through individually, looking up each verse and answering each question.

God's Nature

What do you learn about God's nature in John 3:16?

Our Problem

We are all sinful. Each of us has turned away from a loving and holy God in order to pursue our own interests.

God's Solution

Although sin has become a barrier between us and God, in his great love God has provided a solution. Jesus died on the cross to endure our well-deserved punishment. He died instead of us so that we could be forgiven. Before Jesus died on the cross, God required his people to offer the blood sacrifice of a lamb for forgiveness on a daily basis. But Jesus came as the all-sufficient sacrifice. How significant is John the Baptist's name for Jesus in John 1:29!

The writer of Hebrews tells us, "He [Jesus] then added, 'Here I am. I have come to give my life.' He cancels the first system [the Old Testament sacrificial system] in favor of a far better one. Under this new plan we have been forgiven and made clean by Christ's dying for us once and for all" (Hebrews 10:9-10, TLB).

Our Response

It is not enough for us simply to understand God's plan or to repeat a creed with the facts. Each of us must respond with our whole heart in order to be forgiven and reconciled to God. Our response must show both faith and repentance. First, each of us must recognize that we are sinful, that we need a Savior.

How important is Jesus to our eternal destiny (John 3:36)?

Second, we need to turn away from our sin to Jesus Christ. Then we need to welcome him into our hearts as our Savior and the Lord of our lives.

Read John 1:12. What is God's promise? Have you acted on it?

This is how Acts 20:21 explains why we should respond: "I have had one message for Jews and Gentiles alike—the necessity of turning from sin to God through faith in our Lord Jesus Christ" (TLB).

Is there anything about this Good News that is not clear to you? Share your question with the group.

The remaining questions are for you to answer privately:

Have you ever committed your life to Jesus Christ? If so, who have you told about it? One of the evidences that a new life has begun is that you will want to let someone else know. (Remember the Samaritan woman in John 4.)

If you have not committed your life to Christ, or if you are unsure whether you have, why not do it now and be sure? Tell the Lord you want to turn from your sin and to Jesus Christ. Invite Jesus in to be your Savior and Lord of your life. (Don't worry about the eloquence of your words. God understands your inner thoughts.) Write here what you want to say to him.

If you made this commitment, you are now God's child (John 1:12). You are part of his family!

Who Is a Christian?

ROMANS 1:16–2:4; 3:21-31; 8:1-14

The book of Romans, perhaps more clearly than any other New Testament book, explains the gospel and answers the question, "Who is a Christian?" It contains key passages on the nature of our separation from God (sin) and our way back to God (salvation).

The teacher and apostle Paul had never met the Roman Christians when he wrote this letter. Perhaps that is why he so carefully explained points of the faith—he could not teach his listeners face to face and wanted to be very clear. Believers ever since have benefited from this letter, which deals with faith both in theory and in practice.

1. Imagine that you are a radio broadcaster surveying people at random. List some of the responses you would get to the question, "What makes a person a Christian?"

READ ROMANS 1:16-17 (TLB).

[16]For I am not ashamed of this Good News about Christ. It is God's powerful method of bringing all who believe it to heaven. This message was preached first to the Jews alone, but now everyone is invited to come to God in this same way. [17]This Good News tells us that God makes us ready for heaven—makes us right in God's sight—when we put our faith and trust in Christ to save us. This is accomplished from start to finish by faith. As the Scripture says it, "The man who finds life will find it through trusting God."

2. Why might some people be ashamed to tell others the Good News?

Why wasn't Paul ashamed of it?

3. Who makes us "right in God's sight"?

READ ROMANS 1:18-32 (TLB).

[18]But God shows his anger from heaven against all sinful, evil men who push away the truth from them. [19]For the truth about God is known to them instinctively; God has

put this knowledge in their hearts. [20]Since earliest times men have seen the earth and sky and all God made, and have known of his existence and great eternal power. So they will have no excuse [when they stand before God at Judgment Day].

[21]Yes, they knew about him all right, but they wouldn't admit it or worship him or even thank him for all his daily care. And after awhile they began to think up silly ideas of what God was like and what he wanted them to do. The result was that their foolish minds became dark and confused. [22]Claiming themselves to be wise without God, they became utter fools instead. [23]And then, instead of worshiping the glorious, ever-living God, they took wood and stone and made idols for themselves, carving them to look like mere birds and animals and snakes and puny men.

[24]So God let them go ahead into every sort of sex sin, and do whatever they wanted to—yes, vile and sinful things with each other's bodies. [25]Instead of believing what they knew was the truth about God, they deliberately chose to believe lies. So they prayed to the things God made, but wouldn't obey the blessed God who made these things.

[26]That is why God let go of them and let them do all these evil things, so that even their women turned against God's natural plan for them and indulged in sex sin with each other. [27]And the men, instead of having a normal sex relationship with women, burned with lust for each other, men doing shameful things with other men and, as a result, getting paid within their own souls with the penalty they so richly deserved.

[28]So it was that when they gave God up and would not even acknowledge him, God gave them up to doing everything their evil minds could think of. [29]Their lives became full of every kind of wickedness and sin, of greed and hate, envy, murder, fighting, lying, bitterness, and gossip.

[30]They were backbiters, haters of God, insolent, proud, braggarts, always thinking of new ways of sinning and continually being disobedient to their parents. [31]They tried to misunderstand, broke their promises, and were heartless—without pity. [32]They were fully aware of God's death penalty for these crimes, yet they went right ahead and did them anyway, and encouraged others to do them, too.

4. Why should everyone know about the existence and power of God?

5. Instead of honoring God, what did people do? How did God judge their wickedness?

What kind of warning do you see in this?

6. What are some human characteristics described in verses 29-31? Which of these apply to you, if any?

READ ROMANS 2:1-4 (TLB).

[1]"Well," you may be saying, "what terrible people you have been talking about!" But wait a minute! You are just as bad. When you say they are wicked and should be punished, you are talking about yourselves, for you do these very same things. [2]And we know that God, in justice, will punish anyone who does such things as these. [3]Do you think that God will judge and condemn others for doing them and overlook you when you do them, too? [4]Don't you realize how patient he is being with you? Or don't you care? Can't you see that he has been waiting all this time without punishing you, to give you time to turn from your sin? His kindness is meant to lead you to repentance.

7. If you are about to judge others for their sins, what does Paul say to you about this in Romans 2:1?

↗ 8. Because God has not yet punished you, perhaps you feel you must not be particularly sinful. What did Paul say about this in Romans 2:4? Using a dictionary, define *repentance.*

Read Romans 3:21-31 (tlb).

21, 22But now God has shown us a different way to heaven—not by "being good enough" and trying to keep his laws, but by a new way (though not new, really, for the Scriptures told about it long ago). Now God says he will accept and acquit us—declare us "not guilty"—if we trust Jesus Christ to take away our sins. And we all can be saved in this same way, by coming to Christ, no matter who we are or what we have been like. 23Yes, all have sinned; all fall short of God's glorious ideal; 24yet now God declares us "not guilty" of offending him if we trust in Jesus Christ, who in his kindness freely takes away our sins.

25For God sent Christ Jesus to take the punishment for our sins and to end all God's anger against us. He used Christ's blood and our faith as the means of saving us from his wrath. In this way he was being entirely fair, even though he did not punish those who sinned in former times. For he was looking forward to the time when Christ would come and take away those sins. 26And now in these days also he can receive sinners in this same way, because Jesus took away their sins.

But isn't this unfair for God to let criminals go free, and say that they are innocent? No, for he does it on the basis of their trust in Jesus who took away their sins. [27]Then what can we boast about doing, to earn our salvation? Nothing at all. Why? Because our acquittal is not based on our good deeds; it is based on what Christ has done and our faith in him. [28]So it is that we are saved by faith in Christ and not by the good things we do.

[29]And does God save only the Jews in this way? No, the Gentiles, too, may come to him in this same manner. [30]God treats us all the same; all, whether Jews or Gentiles, are acquitted if they have faith. [31]Well then, if we are saved by faith, does this mean that we no longer need to obey God's laws? Just the opposite! In fact, only when we trust Jesus can we truly obey him.

9. Though our sin has separated us from God, what Good News does Paul tell us in Romans 3:24-25?

How does Christ's death on the cross display the holiness and justice of God? How does it display his love?

10. Since salvation is a free gift from God, does that
     mean we can live as we please and still be sure of
     heaven (Romans 3:31)? What should follow trust
     in Jesus?

Read Romans 8:1-14 (tlb).

¹So there is now no condemnation awaiting those who
belong to Christ Jesus. ²For the power of the life-giving
Spirit—and this power is mine through Christ Jesus—has
freed me from the vicious circle of sin and death. ³We
aren't saved from sin's grasp by knowing the commandments of God, because we can't and don't keep them, but
God put into effect a different plan to save us. He sent his
own Son in a human body like ours—except that ours are
sinful—and destroyed sin's control over us by giving himself as a sacrifice for our sins. ⁴So now we can obey God's
laws if we follow after the Holy Spirit and no longer obey
the old evil nature within us.

⁵Those who let themselves be controlled by their
lower natures live only to please themselves, but those
who follow after the Holy Spirit find themselves doing
those things that please God. ⁶Following after the Holy
Spirit leads to life and peace, but following after the old
nature leads to death, ⁷because the old sinful nature
within us is against God. It never did obey God's laws and
it never will. ⁸That's why those who are still under the
control of their old sinful selves, bent on following their
old evil desires, can never please God.

⁹But you are not like that. You are controlled by your new nature if you have the Spirit of God living in you. (And remember that if anyone doesn't have the Spirit of Christ living in him, he is not a Christian at all.) ¹⁰Yet, even though Christ lives within you, your body will die because of sin; but your spirit will live, for Christ has pardoned it. ¹¹And if the Spirit of God, who raised up Jesus from the dead, lives in you, he will make your dying bodies live again after you die, by means of this same Holy Spirit living within you.

¹²So, dear brothers, you have no obligations whatever to your old sinful nature to do what it begs you to do. ¹³For if you keep on following it you are lost and will perish, but if through the power of the Holy Spirit you crush it and its evil deeds, you shall live. ¹⁴For all who are led by the Spirit of God are sons of God.

11. What wonderful promise is given in Romans 8:1 to those who have trusted Christ?

12. What help do we receive in following God's ways rather than our evil nature (verse 4)? Give an example of this verse in action.

13. Contrast the life of someone who is controlled by his or her lower nature with the life of someone who is obeying the Holy Spirit.

14. Give examples of times or situations when you might be sensitive to the Holy Spirit's prompting to trust him and obey him.

15. According to verse 9, who is a Christian? What else will the Spirit do for us, according to verse 11?

The Christian's Identity and Purpose

1 PETER 1:18-25; 2:9-12

P eter, like John, was very close to Jesus, one of his inner circle. In his second letter Peter said, "We did not follow cleverly invented stories when we told you about the power and coming of our Lord Jesus Christ, but we were eyewitnesses of his majesty" (2 Peter 1:16).

In Peter's letters we are made aware not only of the reality and importance of Jesus but also of our own identity and purpose as children of God.

1. What were your earliest aims in life? What kinds of goals did your parents or other family members have that made an impression on you?

Read 1 Peter 1:18-21 (tlb).

[18]God paid a ransom to save you from the impossible road to heaven which your fathers tried to take, and the ransom he paid was not mere gold or silver as you very well know. [19]But he paid for you with the precious lifeblood of Christ, the sinless, spotless Lamb of God. [20]God chose him for this purpose long before the world began, but only recently was he brought into public view, in these last days, as a blessing to you.

[21]Because of this, your trust can be in God who raised Christ from the dead and gave him great glory. Now your faith and hope can rest in him alone.

⌀ 2. Peter said we have been *redeemed* and *ransomed.* Define these words. Use a dictionary if you wish.

What pictures do these words bring to your mind? What price was paid to redeem us (verse 19)?

3. Would you say that the pursuits of a person living apart from God are meaningless or empty? Why?

As you survey your past life, what are some empty pursuits from which you have been redeemed?

4. Although salvation is a free gift to us on the basis of faith, what did it cost Christ (verse 19)? How long ago was Christ chosen to be the sacrifice for our sins (verse 20)?

READ 1 PETER 1:22-25 (TLB).

²²Now you can have real love for everyone because your souls have been cleansed from selfishness and hatred when you trusted Christ to save you; so see to it that you really do love each other warmly, with all your hearts.

²³For you have a new life. It was not passed on to you from your parents, for the life they gave you will fade away. This new one will last forever, for it comes from Christ, God's ever-living Message to men.

²⁴Yes, our natural lives will fade as grass does when it

becomes all brown and dry. All our greatness is like a flower that droops and falls; [25]but the Word of the Lord will last forever. And his message is the Good News that was preached to you.

5. What is one evidence of change in the life of a person who has received Christ (verse 22)?

In your contacts with other Christians, have you experienced this? If so, describe how this love differs from the world's love.

6. Why is the Good News something we can depend on (verse 25)?

If the Word of the Lord is eternal, what effect do you think this has on those who receive it and live by it?

READ 1 PETER 2:9-12 (TLB).

⁹But you are not like that, for you have been chosen by God himself—you are priests of the King, you are holy and pure, you are God's very own—all this so that you may show to others how God called you out of the darkness into his wonderful light. ¹⁰Once you were less than nothing; now you are God's own. Once you knew very little of God's kindness; now your very lives have been changed by it.

¹¹Dear brothers, you are only visitors here. Since your real home is in heaven I beg you to keep away from the evil pleasures of this world; they are not for you, for they fight against your very souls.

¹²Be careful how you behave among your unsaved neighbors; for then, even if they are suspicious of you and talk against you, they will end up praising God for your good works when Christ returns.

7. Peter used four phrases to describe those who have placed their trust in Christ (verse 9). List them and discuss how each one is true of Christians.

Which phrase is the most meaningful to you? Why?

8. In verses 9 and 10, find three contrasts between non-Christians and Christians. How should these verses help believers feel good about themselves and yet protect them from pride?

9. For what purpose has God called believers out of darkness (verse 9)?

John Calvin said that it is the first duty of the Christian to make God's invisible kingdom visible. Think of some specific ways you might show the light and love of God in your family, among your neighbors or co-workers, and in your world.

10. Remember the story of the Samaritan woman (John 4)? Before she met Christ, how might she have answered the question "Who are you and how do you find meaning in life?" How would she have described her identity and purpose after she met Christ?

    How would you answer the question "Who are you and how do you find meaning in life?"

11. How did Peter describe Christians in verse 11? Name several specific values and beliefs held by Christians that would be alien to people in the world and thus be rejected by them.

12. In verse 11, Peter called believers "visitors"—
strangers, sojourners, or temporary residents. As
Christians, our real home is in heaven, and our
thoughts and goals should show that our life is cen-
tered in the spiritual rather than in the material.
With this in mind, list three goals you might set for
yourself this month. (Be specific. For example, a
father might plan to pray with his teenage son before
they leave the house each morning. A single woman
might plan to invite a widow over for supper.)

13. Why is it important for us as Christians to resist sinful desires? What effect do such desires have on us
(verse 11)?

Name some specific situations in which your own
sinful desires weaken you spiritually.

14. In your own words, explain Peter's reason for living a life beyond reproach (verse 12).

15. What have you learned in this study in the past seven weeks that will make a difference in your life?

Leader's Notes

Remember that your goal is to learn all that you can *from the Bible passage being studied.* Let it speak for itself without using Bible commentaries or other Bible passages. There is more than enough in each assigned passage to keep your group productively occupied for one session. Sticking to the passage saves the group from insecurity and confusion.

Every legitimately seeking person is bound to have questions. Nicodemus and the Samaritan woman did. Pray much for your group before you begin. Here are a few ideas that may help you as you respond to questions.

Whatever the question is, always respond in love, keeping in mind that this person may be looking for eternal answers. With compassion in your heart and the fear of God motivating you, be quick to listen and slow to speak, and don't become angry. Having the right answer isn't nearly as important as having the right attitude. If someone in your group loses sight of this, you must try to be a peacemaker.

Difficult questions, such as "What about those people in other places who haven't heard the Good News?" or "Why do the innocent suffer?" may come up. Author Paul Little, in his classic book *How to Give Away Your Faith* (InterVarsity), gave his responses to the seven questions he heard repeatedly when he spoke to students on college campuses. If someone in your group is stumped by a question, you may want to respond, "That's a good but difficult question that calls for some research on the side." You can offer to do some work on it in the following week or ask for volunteers; then set aside some time during the next study—a short segment at the beginning—to share the results of the research. If too many people respond to a question, the asker may feel overwhelmed. Diplomatically move the discussion to the next subject.

If a group member tends to monopolize the discussion and hasn't responded to subtle clues, go to him or her privately and say, "It's important that everyone be heard. I value what you have to say, but I am asking for your help so that the quieter members have time to gather courage to speak up." If you do not do this early, your group will suffer and may even fold.

Place the chairs in as small a circle as possible (a round table is ideal) to encourage intimacy. Large circles or rows of chairs create an atmosphere that can stifle easy exchange among group members.

Study 1: Who Is Jesus?

Question 1. Give time for this question. If necessary, probe with the following questions: "Can you think of a time in the past twenty-four hours when you expressed love to someone? Encouragement? Instruction? Can you summarize what you said and why?"

Question 4. In Genesis 1:26, God said, "Let *us* make man in our image." The pronouns in this passage show the whole Godhead—the Trinity—at work in creation. This, therefore, is a strong statement for the deity of Jesus, setting him apart from other religious leaders.

Question 5. If necessary, amplify the question by saying, "Think about some of Jesus's instructions, such as being faithful in marriage or helping the poor. Can you think of an example of how people misunderstand or resist a particular instruction? And yet, can you also see how these instructions have endured?"

Question 7. Later in John's gospel (John 3:19-20), you will read that some people love darkness because their deeds are evil. They are comfortable in the shadows and do not want the holy light of Jesus to enter their lives.

Question 9. You might help group members discover answers by going through the phrases in John 1:12-13 and asking some of these questions:
- "Received him"—How did those in verse 11 not receive him? (They didn't believe he was the Christ or welcome him into their lives.)
- "Believed"—Does this mean just intellectual assent? (The Greek word connotes trust.)
- "To become"—How is this different than "to be"? (It's a *change* in status.)
- "Human decision or a husband's will"—Who takes the initiative in salvation? (The point here is that we cannot save ourselves; only God can save us.)

Question 11. The life of John the Baptist was foretold in the Old Testament, just as was the life of Jesus. John was to be Jesus's forerunner, preparing the way for people to see Jesus and follow him. Once Jesus had come, John sent his disciples to follow Jesus.

STUDY 2: MORE ABOUT JESUS

Note on John 2:17. The Old Testament prophets made more than three hundred predictions about the coming Messiah that were literally fulfilled in Jesus. The following two examples relate to this passage:

> Zeal for your house consumes me. (Psalm 69:9, written by David about 1000 BC.)

> "See, I will send my messenger, who will prepare the way before me. Then suddenly the Lord you are seeking will come to his temple; the messenger of the covenant, whom you desire, will come," says the LORD Almighty. But who can endure the day of his coming? Who can stand when he appears? For he will be like a refiner's fire or a launderer's soap. (Malachi 3:1-2, written by the prophet Malachi about 500 BC.)

Question 8. It was a premeditated act, not an outburst of temper.

Question 10. J. I. Packer says that the problem of those who refuse to believe in a God of anger is that they are seeing God in man's image. God's anger is never irrational, self-indulgent, or unjustified, like much of human anger. Packer explains: "God's wrath is a right and necessary reaction to objective moral evil.... Would a God who took as much pleasure in evil as He did in good be a good God? Would a God who did not react adversely to evil in His world be morally perfect? Surely not" (J. I. Packer, *Knowing God,* Downers Grove, IL: InterVarsity, 1973, p. 136).

Remember, although God is angry with our sinful lives, he has also, in his love, made forgiveness possible. First Thessalonians 1:10 tells us that "Jesus...rescues us from the coming wrath." Those who accept his life-sacrifice as payment for their sin are forgiven and may approach God without fear.

STUDY 3: JESUS GIVES ETERNAL LIFE

Question 6. A birth is an event; it happens at a specific time. Yet there are steps leading up to it, and after the event there is a lifetime of growth.

Question 8. Did Nicodemus understand what Jesus was saying? We don't know. We are told, however, in John 19:38-42 that Nicodemus was one of the men who wrapped Jesus's crucified body in myrrh and linen and laid it in the tomb. Surely, as Nicodemus had looked up at Jesus on the cross, Jesus's words would have come back to him: "Just as Moses lifted up the snake in the desert, so the Son of Man must be lifted up, that everyone who believes in him may have eternal life" (John 3:14-15).

Question 10. The Greek word *pisteuō,* here translated "believe," goes beyond mere credence. It means to have faith in, to put our trust in, to be committed to. In other words, it is not enough for us to understand and repeat a creed that says Jesus died for our sins. We must respond to the news with repentance (a turning around, a ceasing to sin, a starting to live for Christ) and trust that his death opened up a way for us to be in touch with God.

Question 14. This provides an opportunity for those who have been born again to give a brief testimony. Briefly model your own testimony, sharing one or two examples of how Christ has changed your life.

STUDY 4: JESUS SATISFIES OUR LONGINGS

Question 2. The Samaritan woman had three strikes against her: She was a despised Samaritan, she was a woman, and she had a reputation for immorality.

Question 3. In his conversation with Nicodemus, Jesus compared spiritual birth to physical birth. With the woman at the well, he compared spiritual water to physical water. *Living water* in that culture meant water that moved, like a rushing stream. In John 7:38-39 Jesus explained that spiritual living water comes from the new life the Holy Spirit gives. When a person trusts Christ as Savior and Lord, the Holy Spirit enters and brings new life that is like an internal well of water bubbling up.

STUDY 5: RESPONDING TO JESUS

Question 2. Many archaeological discoveries have confirmed the Bible's descriptions of places and structures. Excavations of a pool near the Sheep Gate have uncovered five porticoes, or covered colonnades.

Question 5. According to the Jewish leaders, carrying a mat on the Sabbath was work, and therefore it broke the law of the Sabbath (Exodus 20:8). God intended the Sabbath rest for good, but the Jewish leaders made it burdensome by their petty interpretations.

Question 8. C. S. Lewis, the renowned Oxford scholar and author, emphasized the importance of examining Jesus's claims. Although Jesus never called himself simply a teacher, many people place him in that category. Lewis wrote:

> This is the one thing we must not say. A man who
> was merely a man and said the sort of things Jesus said
> would not be a great moral teacher. He would either be a
> lunatic—on a level with the man who says he is a poached
> egg—or else he would be the Devil of Hell. You must
> make your choice. Either this man was, and is, the Son of
> God, or else a madman or something worse. You can shut
> Him up for a fool, you can spit at Him and kill Him as a
> demon; or you can fall at His feet and call Him Lord and
> God. But let us not come with any patronizing nonsense
> about His being a great human teacher. He has not left
> that open to us. He did not intend to (*Mere Christianity*,
> New York: Macmillan, 1952, pp. 40-41).

Question 9. The Bible Knowledge Commentary makes the following observation concerning John 5:28-29: "This passage might imply a salvation by good deeds, but a consideration of John's theology as a whole forbids this (cf. John 3:17-21; John 6:28-29). Those who are truly born again do live a different kind of life. They obey Him (John 14:15), they abide in Him (John 15:5-7), and they walk in the light (John 8:12; 1 John 1:7). They are saved by the Lamb of God who, as their substitutionary sacrifice, takes away the penalty of their sin. Salvation is by faith in Christ. Damnation is because of rejection of God's Son (John 3:36)" (Edwin A. Blum, *The Bible Knowledge Commentary,* Wheaton, IL: Victor Books, 1983, p. 291).

Question 12. The Jewish people understood from their prophecies that Jesus's claim to be the Messiah was the same as claiming to be God in the flesh. Further evidence that Jesus is who he claims to be can be found in John 20. The group may want to skim this chapter briefly.

After the last numbered question (question 13) is a short supplemental section, the purpose of which is to state clearly the gospel message and provide questions and directions that can help group members make informed and intentional choices to become Christians.

At this point, each individual in the group needs to decide if he or she will continue in this study. The studyguide *1, 2, 3 John: How Should a Christian Live?* is designed as a follow-up to this studyguide. If you plan to use it, and while you are waiting for the new studyguides to arrive, you can do the two final lessons in this book, which give the perspectives of two other apostles: Paul and Peter.

Additional leader's note: If the group needs more time to consider Jesus and his claims, we suggest that you continue your group study with *Mark: God in Action* by Chuck and Winnie Christensen, followed by *1, 2, 3 John: How Should a Christian Live?*

Study 6: Who Is a Christian?

In these last two studies, the text from *The Living Bible* is used. The Romans passages, in particular, tend to be difficult, and many new Christians find *The Living Bible* helpful. *The Living Bible* is a thought-for-thought paraphrase rather than a word-for-word translation (such as the *New International Version,* which we used for the studies in John). Kenneth Taylor originally paraphrased *The Living Bible* for his children. He took English translations and, with the help of Greek word studies and commentaries, rephrased them in his own words to help his children understand the meaning.

As you develop the habit of spending time in God's Word every day, we suggest you study from a more literal translation. Translations such as the *New International Version* and the *New American Standard Bible* are very accurate because many scholars collaborated, going back to the original Hebrew and Greek and carefully searching for the best words and phrases to relay God's meaning. However, when you are having trouble understanding a passage, you will find *The Living Bible* helpful.

Question 8. It is possible to feel sorry without repenting. Judas was sorry he betrayed Jesus and hung himself, but he didn't repent, for Jesus tells us that Judas was lost. Second Corinthians 7:10 says, "Godly sorrow brings repentance that leads to salvation and leaves no regret, but worldly sorrow brings death."

Question 11. Fritz Ridenour comments: "In far too many circles Christianity has been reduced to another religion, complete with rituals, rules and all necessary accoutrements to 'reach up to God.' But this is not the gospel.... In the gospel, God is saying to man, 'I love you; the burden is off your back. I have reached down to do something for you. Christ died for your sin, your guilt, your inadequacy. And Christ rose again. He lives and if your personal faith is in Him, you live also'" (Fritz

Ridenour, *How to Be a Christian Without Being Religious,* Glendale, CA: Gospel Light, 1967, pp. 6, 8).

Study 7: The Christian's Identity and Purpose

Question 2. In 1 Peter 1:18, the *New International Version* says, "You were redeemed from the empty way of life handed down to you from your forefathers." This is a more accurate rendering of this verse.

In the Old Testament religious system, the sins of people were rectified by the killing of a choice lamb without any imperfections. The sacrificial system was quite detailed—with sin offerings, guilt offerings, thanksgiving offerings, and so on. These were all merely a foreshadowing of how God would ultimately deal with evil, through the life, death, and resurrection of his Son, Jesus Christ. When Jesus was referred to as "the Lamb of God," any Jew would have made the connection immediately. This is one reason Jesus was either accepted or hated. Anyone accepting his claims automatically accepted that the old way of "rightness in God's sight" had been nullified; the old sacrificial system had been replaced by the ultimate Sacrifice.

Question 5. The person who has received Christ as Savior and Lord is going to be different because the Spirit of Christ is living in him or her. As the apostle Peter said, "We have a new life!" When we receive this new life, we are like newborn babies. It is important for us to listen to Peter's instruction: "Like newborn babies, crave pure spiritual milk, so that by it you may grow up in your salvation" (1 Peter 2:2).

What Should We Study Next?

I f you enjoyed this Fisherman Bible Studyguide, you might want to explore our full line of Fisherman Resources and Bible Studyguides. The following books offer time-tested Fisherman inductive Bible studies for individuals or groups.

FISHERMAN RESOURCES

The Art of Spiritual Listening: Responding to God's Voice Amid the Noise of Life by Alice Fryling
Balm in Gilead by Dudley Delffs
The Essential Bible Guide by Whitney T. Kuniholm
Questions from the God Who Needs No Answers: What Is He Really Asking of You? by Carolyn and Craig Williford
Reckless Faith: Living Passionately As Imperfect Christians by Jo Kadlecek
Soul Strength: Spiritual Courage for the Battles of Life by Pam Lau

FISHERMAN BIBLE STUDYGUIDES

Topical Studies
Angels by Vinita Hampton Wright
Becoming Women of Purpose by Ruth Haley Barton
Building Your House on the Lord: A Firm Foundation for Family Life (Revised Edition) by Steve and Dee Brestin

Discipleship: The Growing Christian's Lifestyle by James and
        Martha Reapsome
*Doing Justice, Showing Mercy: Christian Action in Today's
        World* by Vinita Hampton Wright
Encouraging Others: Biblical Models for Caring by Lin Johnson
The End Times: Discovering What the Bible Says by E. Michael
        Rusten
Examining the Claims of Jesus by Dee Brestin
Friendship: Portraits in God's Family Album by Steve and Dee
        Brestin
The Fruit of the Spirit: Cultivating Christlike Character by
        Stuart Briscoe
Great Doctrines of the Bible by Stephen Board
Great Passages of the Bible by Carol Plueddemann
Great Prayers of the Bible by Carol Plueddemann
Growing Through Life's Challenges by James and Martha
        Reapsome
Guidance & God's Will by Tom and Joan Stark
Heart Renewal: Finding Spiritual Refreshment by Ruth Goring
Higher Ground: Steps Toward Christian Maturity by Steve and
        Dee Brestin
Images of Redemption: God's Unfolding Plan Through the Bible
        by Ruth E. Van Reken
Integrity: Character from the Inside Out by Ted W. Engstrom
        and Robert C. Larson
Lifestyle Priorities by John White
Marriage: Learning from Couples in Scripture by R. Paul and
        Gail Stevens
Miracles by Robbie Castleman
One Body, One Spirit: Building Relationships in the Church by
        Dale and Sandy Larsen

The Parables of Jesus by Gladys Hunt

Parenting with Purpose and Grace: Wisdom for Responding to Your Child's Deepest Needs by Alice Fryling

Prayer: Discovering What Scripture Says by Timothy Jones and Jill Zook-Jones

The Prophets: God's Truth Tellers by Vinita Hampton Wright

Proverbs and Parables: God's Wisdom for Living by Dee Brestin

Satisfying Work: Christian Living from Nine to Five by R. Paul Stevens and Gerry Schoberg

Senior Saints: Growing Older in God's Family by James and Martha Reapsome

The Sermon on the Mount: A Radical Way of Being God's People by Gladys Hunt

Speaking Wisely: Exploring the Power of Words by Poppy Smith

Spiritual Disciplines: The Tasks of a Joyful Life by Larry Sibley

Spiritual Gifts by Karen Dockrey

Spiritual Hunger: Filling Your Deepest Longings by Jim and Carol Plueddemann

A Spiritual Legacy: Faith for the Next Generation by Chuck and Winnie Christensen

Spiritual Warfare: Disarming the Enemy Through the Power of God by A. Scott Moreau

The Ten Commandments: God's Rules for Living by Stuart Briscoe

Ultimate Hope for Changing Times by Dale and Sandy Larsen

When Faith Is All You Have: A Study of Hebrews 11 by Ruth E. Van Reken

Where Your Treasure Is: What the Bible Says About Money by James and Martha Reapsome

Who Is God? by David P. Seemuth

Who Is Jesus? In His Own Words by Ruth E. Van Reken

Who Is the Holy Spirit? by Barbara H. Knuckles and Ruth E. Van Reken

Wisdom for Today's Woman: Insights from Esther by Poppy Smith

Witnesses to All the World: God's Heart for the Nations by Jim and Carol Plueddemann

Women at Midlife: Embracing the Challenges by Jeanie Miley

Worship: Discovering What Scripture Says by Larry Sibley

Bible Book Studies

Genesis: Walking with God by Margaret Fromer and Sharrel Keyes

Exodus: God Our Deliverer by Dale and Sandy Larsen

Ruth: Relationships That Bring Life by Ruth Haley Barton

Ezra and Nehemiah: A Time to Rebuild by James Reapsome

(For Esther, see Topical Studies, *Wisdom for Today's Woman*)

Job: Trusting Through Trials by Ron Klug

Psalms: A Guide to Prayer and Praise by Ron Klug

Proverbs: Wisdom That Works by Vinita Hampton Wright

Ecclesiastes: A Time for Everything by Stephen Board

Song of Songs: A Dialogue of Intimacy by James Reapsome

Jeremiah: The Man and His Message by James Reapsome

Jonah, Habakkuk, and Malachi: Living Responsibly by Margaret Fromer and Sharrel Keyes

Matthew: People of the Kingdom by Larry Sibley

Mark: God in Action by Chuck and Winnie Christensen

Luke: Following Jesus by Sharrel Keyes

John: An Eyewitness Account of the Son of God by Whitney T. Kuniholm

Acts 1–12: God Moves in the Early Church by Chuck and Winnie Christensen

Acts 13–28 by Chuck and Winnie Christensen (formerly
    titled *Paul: Thirteenth Apostle*)
Romans: The Christian Story by James Reapsome
1 Corinthians: Problems and Solutions in a Growing Church by
    Charles and Ann Hummel
Strengthened to Serve: 2 Corinthians by Jim and Carol
    Plueddemann
Galatians, Titus, and Philemon: Freedom in Christ by Whitney
    Kuniholm
Ephesians: Living in God's Household by Robert Baylis
Philippians: God's Guide to Joy by Ron Klug
Colossians: Focus on Christ by Luci Shaw
Letters to the Thessalonians by Margaret Fromer and Sharrel
    Keyes
Letters to Timothy: Discipleship in Action by Margaret Fromer
    and Sharrel Keyes
Hebrews: Foundations for Faith by Gladys Hunt
James: Faith in Action by Chuck and Winnie Christensen
1 and 2 Peter, Jude: Called for a Purpose by Steve and Dee
    Brestin
1, 2, 3 John: How Should a Christian Live? by Dee Brestin
Revelation: The Lamb Who Is the Lion by Gladys Hunt

Bible Character Studies
Abraham: Model of Faith by James Reapsome
David: Man After God's Own Heart by Robbie Castleman
Elijah: Obedience in a Threatening World by Robbie
    Castleman
Great People of the Bible by Carol Plueddemann
King David: Trusting God for a Lifetime by Robbie
    Castleman

Men Like Us: Ordinary Men, Extraordinary God by Paul
    Heidebrecht and Ted Scheuermann
Moses: Encountering God by Greg Asimakoupoulos
Women Like Us: Wisdom for Today's Issues by Ruth Haley
    Barton
Women Who Achieved for God by Winnie Christensen
Women Who Believed God by Winnie Christensen